BROKEN MARRIAGE

(5) MAJOR FACTORS WHY COUPLES EXPERIENCE FALLOUT IN MARRIAGES

By

DR. MYA GREY

TABLE OF CONTENT

INTRODUCTION

Fairy tales give the illusion of a 'happy ever after' when getting married. Reality check: all married couples experience problems and challenges. Marriage problems can strengthen the relationship of couples if they are committed to spending their lives together and starting a family.

If you're reading this because you're facing a marriage problem, keep reading with an open mind. Explore first what causes your problems so you can come up with solutions on how to fix them. Remember that relationship issues take two to make the marriage work. Sit down and talk with your partner, have open communication, and make the necessary compromise.

CHAPTER 1

INFIDELITY

What Is Infidelity?

Infidelity is also referred to as cheating or adultery is describing the act of engaging in emotional or sexual intimacy with someone outside the agreed-upon boundaries of your marriage or relationship. Infidelity may or may not involve sexual encounters, and can happen in person or online.

Infidelity is, unfortunately, common. Rates of infidelity in relationships vary from about 20% to 50%. Infidelity can have a strong impact on the relationship and can lead to depression, guilt, blame, and anger.

Signs of Infidelity

It can be difficult to know if your partner is cheating on you without concrete evidence. However, there are some warning signs that your spouse may be engaging in infidelity. When it comes to infidelity, there will usually be multiple red flags that clue you into what is going on.

Some potential signs of infidelity include:2

*   You may notice significant changes in your sex life, that your partner is less interested in sex than usual and has trouble becoming sexually aroused with you or that your partner is much more interested in sex with you than they usually are

*   Your partner may want to engage in sexual activities that seem foreign or off-putting to you

*   Your partner may be paying more attention to their appearance than usual

*   Your partner may not be sleeping well

*   Your partner may seem unusually distracted and stressed

*   Your partner may be more private than usual and may demand more privacy

*   Your partner may be spending more time away from home or going on longer and more frequent trips for work or with friends

*   You may find it more difficult to connect with your partner, and they may be more reactive, more hostile, or colder than usual

*   You may also experience sleeplessness stress, and distraction as a result of your suspicion about your partner's behavior

Causes of Infidelity

Many of us have the idea that infidelity only happens in unhappy relationships, but even people in happy relationships cheat. Infidelity often happens because of dissatisfaction within a relationship, but it can also happen because of low self-esteem, or an addiction to sex or romance.3 At other times, it happens because of personality traits, a permissive attitude about sex, and cultural and societal norms about sex and relationships that support infidelity.4

There are some studies that show that men are more likely to cheat than women, but others show that men are more likely to engage in sexual infidelity, whereas women are more likely to engage in emotional infidelity. People with higher sexual urges are more likely to engage in infidelity, as are people with higher levels of insecurity, who may be seeking validation through an affair.

Types of Infidelity

Infidelity doesn't just look like someone going out to a motel and having a secret sexual affair. Cheating can take many forms and doesn't always involve in-person encounters. It's also important to note that what may constitute infidelity for one person may not ring true for another.

For example, while some people consider viewing pornography "cheating," others may view this as normal and acceptable. The point is that each couple should clearly define what is and isn't allowed in their relationship and which activities would constitute a boundary violation.

Sexual Infidelity

This involves engaging in sexual relations of any kind outside of the relationship. There may or may not be an emotional component here.

Emotional Infidelity

The difference between a platonic relationship and a case of emotional infidelity is that the relationship involves flirting, sexual chemistry, and a level of emotional intimacy similar to romantic relationships. Additionally, there is secrecy involved: information about the relationship is often purposefully hidden.

Online Infidelity

Online, or cyber infidelity, involves engaging in sexual or emotional affairs online, via chat rooms, messages, texts, and exchanging of photos and sexual fantasies. Some people consider viewing pornography without engaging with others a type of cheating, while others do not.5 Common Types of Affairs

Impact of Infidelity

Infidelity can have serious impacts on relationships and on the individuals involved, including those who are cheated on, and those who do the cheating. When infidelity impacts a relationship, it can leave the people in it feeling highly distressed, depressed, and out of sorts. It can cause heightened anxiety, suicidal ideation, and signs of post-traumatic stress disorder (PTSD).

The person who was cheated on may feel deeply betrayed, and suspicious of their spouse's activities going forward. They may experience nightmares, flashbacks, and may have images of the affair playing in their head as if on a movie reel. Trust may be severed, and difficult to repair.3

Finally, infidelity can strain or break apart relationships or marriages. Infidelity is one of the top reasons that couples go to relationship counseling, and it's one of the most common reasons for divorce.

CHAPTER 2

DOMESTIC VIOLENCE

Domestic violence is very common in American families. In almost 20 percent of all marriages and intimate partnerships, couples slap, shove, hit, or otherwise assault each other. Emotional abuse verbal threats, humiliating or degrading remarks, and controlling behavior is even more common. If you or someone you love is in an abusive relationship, help is available.

Intimate partner violence is especially common among young couples, and, without intervention, may escalate in intensity or frequency. Relationships are challenging, and some couples deal with conflict by becoming aggressive, controlling and mean. Abuse can begin with subtle actions. For example, otherwise happy couples might lose their tempers, or one might become possessive or critical. This may get ignored or downplayed, but small acts of aggression often lead to more damaging behavior. Sometimes abuse gradually develops into severe violence after couples are marriage or in long-term relationships that are difficult to change. Couples frequently excuse or ignore early aggressive incidents and believe that once current stressors end, the violence will end. However, even minor acts of violence can escalate over time, increasing the risk of injury or even homicide.

There are many types of abusive behavior. One common pattern is distinguished by coercion and control. This can include jealousy, monitoring of behavior, retaliation, and emotional and physical abuse. Controlling abuse is usually called intimate terrorism, and over 90% of the perpetrators are male. In a typical case a husband might prevent a wife from seeing friends or family and make her feel guilty or afraid if she defies him. He may threaten harm against children if she tries to leave, or badger her incessantly to get what he wants.

Another type of violence is characterized by aggression, but little or no controlling behavior. This type, usually referred to as situational couple violence, occurs as disagreements escalate into physical actions such as pushing or slapping. This pattern is more likely to be mutual, and is equally perpetrated by men and women. Although this type of violence is generally less severe than intimate terrorism, it still can devastate a marriage, lead to criminal charges and injuries, and have long-term

negative effects on children.

A purple ribbon is used to promote awareness of domestic violence

In 2015, the United Kingdom's Home Office widened the definition of domestic violence to include coercive control.

Globally, the victims of domestic violence are overwhelmingly women, and women tend to experience more severe forms of violence. The World Health Organization (WHO) estimates 1 in 3 of all women are subject to domestic violence at some point in their life. They are also likelier than men to use intimate partner violence in self-defense. In some countries, domestic violence may be seen as justified or legally permitted, particularly in cases of actual or suspected infidelity on the part of the woman. Research has established that there exists a direct and significant correlation between a country's level of gender equality and rates of domestic violence, where countries with less gender equality experience higher rates of domestic violence.

Domestic violence is among the most underreported crimes worldwide for both men and women. In addition, due to social stigmas regarding male victimization, men who are victims of domestic violence face an increased likelihood of being overlooked by healthcare providers

Domestic violence often occurs when the abuser believes that they are entitled to it, or that it is acceptable, justified, or unlikely to be reported. It may produce an intergenerational cycle of violence in children and other family members, who may feel that such violence is acceptable or condoned. Many people do not recognize themselves as abusers or victims, because they may consider their experiences as family conflicts that had gotten out of control. Awareness, perception, definition and documentation of domestic violence differs widely from country to country. Additionally, domestic violence often happens in the context of forced or child marriages.

In abusive relationships, there may be a cycle of abuse during which tensions rise and an act of violence is committed, followed by a period of reconciliation and calm. The victims may be trapped in domestically violent situations through isolation, power and control, traumatic bonding to the abuser, cultural acceptance, lack of financial resources, fear, and shame, or to protect children. As a result of abuse, victims may experience physical disabilities, dysregulated aggression, chronic health problems, mental illness, limited finances, and a poor ability to create healthy relationships. Victims may experience severe psychological disorders, such as post-traumatic stress disorder (PTSD). Children who live in a household with violence often show psychological problems from an early age, such as avoidance, hypervigilance to threats and dysregulated aggression, which may contribute to vicarious traumatization.

CHAPTER 3

FINANCIAL INSTABILTY

L, is for the way you look at me. **O**, is for overcoming financial issues in a marriage.

Making a marriage last can take effort even if both spouses are millionaires. Add in money problems, and things can get difficult fast. We've talked before about how one spouse's credit could lead to problems, but that's just one way finances can throw a wrench into a relationship.

That's why it's important to be aware of the kind of problems that can arise, and the methods you can use, as a couple, to overcome them. We spoke to the experts to find out why couples fight over finances, the kind of struggles that come up, and how you can beat them and make sure that love prevails in the end with these money and marriage tips.

Values, in all senses of the word.

It's important to understand where financial struggles in marriage come from so you can try and head them off before they ever come up, or at least have a head start on addressing them.

"Most financial issues in marriage come down to one main factor: both partners have different core values about money," certified counselor and creator of The Popular Man Jonathan Bennett explained. "And, many of these financial values developed very early and are difficult to change. For example, one partner might have been raised to value saving and investing. The other partner might have been taught to indulge his or her whims even if it means living paycheck to paycheck.

"It's very difficult for partners who view money, saving, and spending in fundamentally conflicting ways to manage household finances successfully as a team."

Writer and speaker Frederick Towels agreed about this foundational concern: "Financial issues can most certainly affect a marriage negatively. One of the biggest financial issues that can negatively impact a marriage is how each spouse handles and views money. Each spouse may have different views of money, one spouse may primarily seek to save money for a rainy day and another could have a spending fetish. This type of conflict will typically raise trust issues in the relationship. The difference in philosophies in money can spill over into other areas of the relationship if both spouses aren't careful."

Couples may even have differing ideas about who the money they have belongs to. "Some spouses freely pool their money and treat it as a joint asset," Steven Yoda, a partner with the divorce firm Walzer Melcher, told us. "Other spouses, rightly or wrongly, consider their earnings 'their' money and split expenses down the middle. Some spouses are comfortable with debt, while others are averse to it.

"Oftentimes, these issues are not fully discussed before marriage or even after marriage. This can lead to years of misunderstanding, which reach a boiling point during a divorce. It is easy to see how, in the absence of communication, one spouse may believe that the marital finances are perfectly fine, while the other may be stewing in resentment."

CHAPTER 4

INFERTILITY

In the book of Genesis, we find God's first commandment to humankind: "Be fruitful and multiply. . ." (Genesis 1:28) It appears that God infused this commandment to procreate into the fiber of our beings. It seems to be written in our hearts, dreamed of in our minds, ached for in our bodies, and yearned for in our spirits. Thus, when a couple is unable to have children, it causes great pain emotionally, intellectually, physically, and spiritually. The feelings of emptiness and loss are overwhelming. The search for reasons and remedies becomes a relentless passion. Doctors, procedures, the time, the cost, the hope, and the hurt are constant companions on the lonely road walked by couples searching for the destination of parenthood.

Statistics tell us that couples do not walk this road alone. According to the United States Centers for Disease Control (2015), one out of every five couples in America suffers from infertility problems. This means in the United States, 7.3 million women and their partners, of childbearing years, are infertile. Infertility affects the male or female reproductive system with almost equal frequency. Infertility affects people from every racial, ethnic, religious, and socioeconomic level.

Infertility is defined as the inability to conceive within one year of trying, or not being able to carry a child to live birth. Infertility may occur in a couple's first attempts to bring a child into the world, or as secondary infertility when they have successfully given birth before, but are not able to do so again. Women who are able to get pregnant, but have miscarriages, are also said to be infertile.

Keep in mind that there are as many roads to resolving infertility as there are infertile couples to travel them. The array of options and medical interventions for a couple facing fertility challenges can be confusing and hazardous. Each route brings many ethical, moral, spiritual, emotional, and physical ramifications. It is important to plan carefully to avoid potholes and ensure a safe trip.

In many climes all over the world, women are handed the wrong end of the stick, when finding the culprits of childlessness in marriages. And in pursuit of finding solutions to this, many women have contributed to the booming businesses of religious centers, herbalists' homes and diviners' coves. Meanwhile, the men folks live in the foolery of the belief that the faults can never be theirs, insomuch, they could function well between the sheets. However, this assertion, medically speaking, is far from the truth.

Infertility in marriage generally refers to when a man and a woman engaged in unprotected sex, at a frequent interval, for over a year and the woman is unable to conceive. It is seen in approximately one in every six couples willing to conceive. Many researches, in different parts of the world, have shown that factors originating from men contribute at least 50% to cases of infertility diagnosed among couples. A man, and not only women, is therefore automatically a suspect, when his wife is not pregnant after a year of marriage, when regular sexual intercourse has taking place.

Many factors contribute to make infertility. Some of these include varicoceles, which refers to the enlargement of veins in the testicles of men that cause overheating, which may affect the number or shape of the sperm. Also, injuries to the testes are known to affect sperm production thereby lowering the number of sperm. Infertility is also commonly seen in people with history of undescended testicle(s).

Other unsavory habits such as smoking, heavy alcohol use or the use of hard drugs are also known to affect the testicular and ejaculatory function of men. So, also are the uses of certain medications and supplements, cancer treatment with certain chemotherapies, radiation and surgeries done to remove one or both testicles. Medical conditions, such as diabetes, cystic fibrosis, some auto-immune disorders and certain infections can also cause testicular failure.

Hormonal disorders in men such as improper hypothalamus or pituitary glands functions may end up in low or no sperm production. So also, are conditions such as pituitary cancers, congenital adrenal hyperplasia, exposure to a lot of estrogen or testosterone, Cushing's syndrome and prolonged use of glucocorticoids. Genetic causes such as Klinefelter's syndrome, Y-chromosome micro-deletion, myotonic dystrophy and some other genetic disorders have also been inculpated in no or low sperm production.

The risk of male infertility is higher in men that are over 40 years old, obese and overweight, and in those smoking, excessively consuming alcohol, smoking marijuana, using testosterone, on irradiation treatment, exposing the testes to high temperatures. Some medications like spironolactone, cimetidine, ketoconazole, bicalutamide, glutamine or cyproterone and exposure to pesticides, mercury, lead or cadmium can also confer a risk of male infertility.

Since it is often cheaper and easier to investigate infertility in men than in a woman, men rather than women should be the first to be investigated when infertility is being suspected in a marriage. A semen analysis that determines the sperm volume, pH, sperm concentration, total sperm count, sperm velocity, linearity, color, and viscosity may be done. Also, this may be followed by a detailed sperm analysis to determine the viability, morphology, and motility of the sperm.

CHAPTER 5

TIME COMMITMENT ISSUES

Distance makes the heart grow fonder, but not too much space and time apart. Time spent away from each other and time spent together are essential for maintaining a healthy marriage.

When couples know how to balance their time with each other, it could result in beautiful opportunities for growth and harmony. What causes a marriage to fail is when couples have trouble balancing their time together.

Sometimes, couples' work and home schedules are not always compatible, leading to ongoing tension in their marriage if not resolved early. Little to no quality time spent together puts severe stress on a marriage and has some spouses contemplating divorce, especially if they're always alone.

Communicating with one's spouse about the quality time they'd like to spend with each other could be an excellent way to address daily routines or work schedules that might impact how much time a couple spends with each other.

Married couples can also partake in different activities that they have in common as a way to reconnect and spend time together.